DOLLARS FLOW TO ME EASILY

Dollars Flow To Me Easily

Richard Dotts

© Richard Dotts 2015 / 2016
1st print edition
ISBN- 13: 9781532736230
ISBN- 10: 1532736231
Questions / comments? The author can be contacted at
RichardDotts@gmail.com

TABLE OF CONTENTS

Chapter One
Welcoming Easy Change into Your Life

This is a book which I have wanted to write for the longest time. While the book *appears* to be about money, financial freedom, and abundance, it is actually about so much more than that. This book is really about the process of change, and more specifically, allowing easy and effortless changes in your life.

As I look back, I can broadly group the changes that occurred in my life into two categories. Changes in the first category were easy and effortless. They happened spontaneously with no effort or willpower on my part. Things just *happened*. It was as if I was the neutral observer throughout the whole process, enjoying and being amazed by change as it happened. It was a beautiful process of metamorphosis for me.

Changes in the second category, however, were a different story. They were arduous and difficult. The change process was challenging. It felt like I was working against the grain all the time, struggling to be someone different from who I was. I struggled to change. Immense willpower, effort and concentration were needed. The change process took time. It took a while before the desired results started to show.

What is the difference between the first and second type of change that occurred in my life? Some people may be tempted to answer that it was the subject matter, the *nature* of the change that took place. We view certain changes in our lives as "big" changes that take a long time to happen. Losing weight or achieving some giant goal (such as financial freedom) commonly fall into this category. Other changes, such as decorating the house or getting a cup of coffee are seen as easy, effortless changes. The purpose of this book is to turn this notion right on its head. I'm here to show you that all changes (regardless of their nature) can be easy and effortless if you allow them to be and work in accordance with greater Universal Laws.

Let me explain with a personal example. Most people struggle with exercising, losing weight and getting fit, but this was a transition that I eased into easily. The catalyst for change came one day when I fell at work. Thankfully, while I sustained no injuries from that painful encounter, my fall made me realize that I was neglecting my overall fitness. It prompted me to take action and the Universe supported me beautifully in my new endeavor. A few days later, the exercise equipment I ordered online was delivered to my house, and I have kept at my exercise routine ever since, working out for 45 minutes on most days despite my schedule. I am still amazed by the ease of it all. I have never once had to struggle with issues of willpower or with any conflicting feelings within myself. I easily stepped into the new desired reality of a fitter me once I set the intention to do it.

On the other hand, achieving financial freedom was a difficult change for me. I struggled with each step along the way, first with curbing my urge to overspend and with the willpower required to work out a budget and stick to it. Then I struggled with all the conflicting feelings of worry, blame, worthiness and guilt that I heaped onto myself. Why did the process seem so easy for everyone else except me? Why could my friends all handle a budget well while I could not? Why can other people stop worrying about money but not me? I spent many years mired in this form of self-critical thinking before I finally stepped out of it.

Over the years, I realized that the goal of financial freedom is the ultimate goal for people in our modern society. This is natural since money has become synonymous with a good life and with the various things we can do with it. Without money to do whatever we want, we feel restricted in our enjoyment of life. I certainly understand what it feels like to be worried about money all the time, worrying about whether we can have enough to enjoy a good meal or the fun experience we so desire. I understand how restricting it feels to be worried about money all the time, which is why I have decided to write this series of books.

As I worked with individuals over the years, I realized that achieving financial independence probably ranks at the top in terms of perceived difficulty. If you asked people to rate how difficult each of their goals were, you would find that "earning money" and "becoming rich" rate amongst the most difficult. Why is that so? We have all been conditioned by society and by our parents to believe that making money is difficult and that it is somehow bad to have lots of money. There is so much emotional baggage associated with the subject of money that all this affects our vibrations when we actually try to manifest it. Without dealing with the contradictory vibrations effectively, we will never address the cause of the problem and create lasting manifestation success.

I have often taught that what we consider to be the "problem" or the "issue" is seldom the real issue in itself. For example, while we may perceive "money" to be the root cause of the problem, it is rarely the true cause. Most of us do not have any issue with money itself, with the very pieces of paper and metal we are trying to ultimately manifest. Many of us, however, have truckloads full of contradictory beliefs and vibrations surrounding the **subject *of*** money. We all have set up certain expectations for ourselves, regarding how easy (or difficult) it would be to earn this money, the means through which we can acquire it and what other people would think about us if we had it. All of these create actual impediments and obstacles when manifesting money. If one has a way to deal with these obstacles (or sticking points) that stand between themselves and their manifestations, their desired reality will come into being very, very quickly!

As I look back at how I manifested a fitter me, I realize that the topic of exercising is one which I have very little emotional baggage on. This is also the same reason why I have paid little attention to this part of my life in the past. So in a way, whatever little attention I paid to this aspect of my life helped, because when I finally decided to "change" this part of my life, there were no old beliefs that I had to overcome. I did not have long-held beliefs about how easy or difficult the process was going to be, or how logical it was to ask for what I wanted. I freed myself from all rules and all expectations.

Think about how it would be like to live in a Universe where you freed yourself from all expectations, rules and beliefs about money. Would you be able to manifest riches and financial abundance at will? Definitely! Would you be able to manifest them in an instant, faster than the time it takes to read this sentence? Of course! I am even willing to wager that in your Universe right now, there are certain areas of your life in which this principle is working out beautifully.

Think of an area in your life where change happens effortlessly, a particular area where you can just decide to have something and "make it happen" with minimal fuss. This is the feeling of *ease* and *flow* that I am talking about here. If it can happen in one

area of your life, then why not in every single area...
including the area of finances?

There are two ways in which people often get
stuck and tripped up by a recurring issue in their
life. The first, as we have addressed earlier, is their
deeply embedded belief that the situation is "difficult to change," or that change will be difficult.
For example, they may erroneously believe that
just because they've had the problem for so long,
or just because everyone *else* thinks it is a difficult
problem...that the same must apply to them as well.
Look at how society views the treatment of certain
diseases. We have all formed societal expectations
about how some diseases are easy to "cure" while
others are incurable. All of these societal "norms"
and expectations go on to affect our vibrations, and
hence our outcome.

The second way in which individuals trip themselves up is by their continued focus on the problem
or issue. They keep talking about it, telling others
about it and analyzing it over-and-over again in their
minds. Their reasons for operating in this manner,
of course, seem completely valid. When I worried
about my finances in the past, I too, saw a need to
worry continually about them in an attempt to find
solutions for them. "Of course I have to worry about
my finances, I am finding a solution to the problem!"
was a common excuse I used to rationalize my worrying. But understand that therein lies the biggest
irony—Your continued operation in "problem-solving" mode is what <u>perpetuates</u> the problem in the

first place. Your continued fixation *on* the problem is what causes it to persist consistently in your reality. This is probably the hardest part for most people to get, but once you understand it, the solution is obvious.

Sometimes, the best way to solve a problem is to stop thinking about it and to think about something else completely. If you can train yourself to do so, then what you'll find (as I've written about so many times) is that the issue resolves itself automatically. The issue ceases to become so big of an issue in your life, and it stops bothering you as much. But most people have trouble operating in this manner (even though it is in line with the highest Universal truths) because they have not functioned in this way before. They have been taught all through their lives that the way to "solve" a problem is to tackle it head-on, to think about it relentlessly, and to take a bull by its horns. Understand that this way of functioning, when it comes to handling many of life's long-standing issues, is actually counterproductive and unnecessary.

For the first ten years in which I was a student of these metaphysical principles, I frequently tried to "solve" the problems or "correct" the issues in my life through the use of everything I had learned. When things worked, the results were sporadic, and things usually returned to their old state a few days or weeks later. This form of regression is common in beginner students of this material, no matter what subject matter we are dealing with. Why is that so?

When a regression occurs, when there is a recurring pattern in your life, it points to the existence of some form of unconscious belief that you are holding on to. These unconscious beliefs are the root cause of the issue, which is continually causing you to think, feel and react in a certain way...which only leads to a continued perpetuation of the issue.

Sometimes, this form of operating in the world can be so entrenched that we do not even realize we are acting in this manner, day in and day out! If someone had told me I was acting unconsciously in certain parts of my life, I would have brushed them off! I shared several anecdotes in my book *Banned Money Secrets*, which talks about various ways in which you can apply manifestation principles to the specific subject of manifesting more money in your life.

My focus for this book is somewhat different. This is a book that **changes you as you read it**. In fact, this is the first book I have written in this manner, which is why I want you to read it with your **heart** rather than with your **head**. Try to focus less on the physical words I use and more on the spiritual essence of what I am trying to convey. Be cognizant that when we are dealing with intangible and timeless spiritual principles, there may not be adequate physical words or expressions to convey what I mean. Therefore, what I have done here (as with many other spiritual teachers) is to use the closest physical equivalent words and phrases, even going to the extent of *inventing* certain words to explain certain concepts when needed. Words such as "manifestative state" and "manifestor" are words that have come to me in the past as I tried to convey certain concepts, and I trust that your higher self will spontaneously understand what I am trying to say as you read them.

What I have done for this book is to set an intention that the <u>highest and best</u> is done for each reader, according to the circumstances in your life with regards to money. In writing this book, I have invited the Universe to write it with me and to express / convey whatever is necessary through me for the fulfillment of your highest good. I have also requested that the Universe convey this information not only through words but also *beyond the level* of physical words. Therefore, as you read this book, one part of you will be picking up on the logical meaning of what I am trying to convey. Your rational mind will be processing the arguments which I make. But the larger part of you (your higher self) will also be receiving intangible information (or energetic vibrations) that is just right for you. I intend that you receive the highest and best, in line with what is needed to manifest financial abundance in your life.

As a scientific person, I used to shun any form of non-verbal communication *until* I realized their significance in our lives. While verbal communications form a large part of our language and our interactions with others, the great spiritual masters have always taught that non-verbal communication exists as well. This means that we are often picking up on the thoughts and intentions of others whether we realize it or not. Your mind is like a transmitter and a receiver of frequencies, and it is receiving *and* transmitting information whether you are conscious of this or otherwise. When pieces of information spontaneously pop up in your mind and appear in your awareness, understand that they may have come from the Universe. A larger part of us is always communicating and at one with the Universal mind.

I encourage you to experience all this for yourself as you read this book. As you are reading it, I encourage you to try to achieve nothing in particular. Give up all your goals or desires. Give up your need to solve any problems in your life. Give up your need to "try" and find a solution. Give up the need to do something. Give up the need to do the right thing or find the right way. Give all of that up.

Instead, in the time that we are together, let your mind wander as you read this book. Let it think about whatever it pleases. Let your body do whatever it pleases. Read this book in the utmost state of relaxation and ease, not wanting to go somewhere else or do something to make something happen. Read it with a completely relaxed state of mind, at peace and at ease with wherever you are at this moment in your life. Where you are right now is exactly where you need to be in your life.

And if you'll begin reading in this non-reactive state and *remain* in this non-reactive state, you may find certain answers or paths spontaneously lighting up for you. You will be given clear impulses or clear directions to turn towards. You will be given crystal clear nudges by the Universe. The resulting changes will be easy and effortless. But don't *force* any of it. Nothing ever comes through force or exertion or trying to control. If you can force your way through everything, then you would have forced your way through the situation and obtained whatever it is that you wanted. So ease off and let go of the need to force your will on anything. Let go of the need to surrender as well. There is neither the need to force nor the need to surrender. Instead, just *be who you are. Be right where you are* as you read this book. You are not reading this book to "solve" a particular problem in your life; you are reading this book to **feel good now.**

And if you can remain in this manifestative state, then you would have transformed by the end of this book...with no effort needed at all on your part. You would have stepped into your natural goodness, in which dollars flow to you easily.

Chapter Two
Your Field of Goodness

Have you ever picked up a spiritual book, only to realize that it wasn't written for who you were at that time? Perhaps the book was too advanced for you, and you needed some help getting started. Or perhaps the book assumed that you were a beginner, and you felt the need to skip through lots of the basic material.

This will not be the case here because you are not trying to "achieve" anything by reading this book. This is a book meant to *change* and transform you at a deep, inner level as you read...and it does not do so through mental coercion or logic. It does not do so through persuasive rhetoric. Instead, what this book does is to guide you to release more and more of your resistance surrounding the subject of money as you read it. We all have unknowingly picked up resistance and certain ways of thinking in our daily lives. Our resistance causes all those negative feelings when we think about money. When the resistance is gone from within us, then not only will the negative feelings be gone...but so will our perceived "problems" and "issues" surrounding money.

As you read this book, drop any notion that you have an "issue" or "problem" with finances that needs to be solved. Thinking that you have a problem is a large part of the problem itself. Instead, focus on your *current* well-being. We are not here to solve any problems. It is not the intention of this book to solve any problems. Instead, the purpose of this book is to change how you think and feel about money. When you can get to that magical place of feeling good, that is when things will start happening for you.

There are so many things which you can focus upon right now as you read this book. First, you may become aware that you have the time to read this book. You have the freedom to decide how to spend your time and what actions you would like to pursue. That is the ultimate freedom which no one can take away from you. Second, you may be aware that you are reading this book in your favorite chair or the favorite spot in your house. Feel how comfortable this place is for you. Feel how safe you feel right here in this moment. This familiar reading spot is always one which you can return to, time and time again. I love to do my reading in a few places around the house. Each of those places is sacred to me for a reason. When I need to do my deepest thinking or spend some time with myself, I retreat to one of these spots away from the outside world. I encourage you to do the same. See the time you spend reading this book as sacred time with your higher self. You are not sitting there "doing nothing" or engaged in fantasy. You are having an important conversation with your higher self.

Most of us are so concerned with worldly issues and problems that we rarely turn inwards. We are so focused on "solving the problem" or "finding a solution to the problem" that we operate in a very outer-directed mode. But what if the answers to life are not found out there? What if all the answers to life are found *within you?* I encourage you to ponder this possibility. If the answers to life can be found *outside* of ourselves in all our worldly knowledge, then those who study the most would have found it. The scholars of our world would be the happiest people in the world. Those who know the most would be leading the most fulfilling lives. But are they? I encourage you to ponder the possibility that the answers we seek lie within each of us.

Give up the need to search on the outside for your answers. This lifelong search for something "outside of ourselves" causes people to be unable to sit still or to enjoy their lives for even one moment. Even if they achieved all their financial goals, they are worried about losing it or obsessed with earning more. Is that true abundance? What is true abundance?

When you realize that you can connect with the essence of true abundance *in any moment*...then not only will the dollars not matter to you, but they'll also flow to you in large amounts. That is the whole irony of it all—When you finally give up the need for something, what you were so *needful* for previously starts flowing to you in huge quantities. But you would no longer react to it in the same way with lust. You would react to this newfound reality in your life with grace and poise.

Just for now, I would like to invite you to connect with the essence of true abundance in your life. Initially, your ego mind may object. The most common objection or excuse it throws up is, "This is a silly exercise! Everything is just happening in the mind. It is not real!" For those of you who have been giving in to the ego mind (or rather, feeding it) for a longer period, it may say, "What's the use of doing all these mental exercises? Nothing in the real world is going to change; your financial situation is certainly not going to change!"

Therein lies the mistaken belief of the ego mind. The ego mind does not know Universal Truth. It only knows lack and limitation. It only knows scarcity. It only knows what society and the individual self has programmed it to know over the years. Therefore, when the ego mind says these mental exercises are "not real," it does not know better. It is not speaking the Truth. All it is merely doing is regurgitating pieces of faulty programming which it has been replaying for you over-and-over again. The biggest irony is that what the ego mind feeds you is just as untrue or unreal. It is constantly offering you false thoughts that *seem* real based on our faulty understanding of the world. (An acronym for FEAR is False Emotions Appearing Real.) That is why in the beginning, you must push ahead regardless of your mind chatter. Just gently let it go.

Ignoring your mind chatter, you settle down and decide to connect with the essence of true abundance within you. Close your eyes and just *feel* abundant. A very light intention is all you need here. Remember—When living these spiritual principles, all you need is a *very* light touch, and the Universe responds spontaneously and beautifully. Force plays no part in any of this. You do not have to "force" the Universe to give you anything. You do not have to "force" the Universe to respond. The need to use force comes when you believe you will not always get what you want, and therefore have to try all ways and means to get it. This is again our faulty logic at work. All of the Universe is always equally present at all times for you. There is no need to "force" energy to flow, it just *is*. You are immersed in the Universal field whether you know it or not. Trying to "force" your Universal good is like standing in a beautiful field of marigolds and then "forcing" the flowers to come to you. That's absurd because the flowers are already here and in full bloom all around you! You just need to open your eyes to see them.

Similarly, all you need to do is to open your inner eyes to recognize the inherent abundance that is already here. Right now, you are standing in a beautiful field of flowers. The flowers are there, but you cannot see them. Why is that so? We are so busy looking on the outside (for certain people, circumstances and methods which we believe can help us achieve our goals) that we hardly take the time to turn inwards. When you turn inwards, you realize that what you have been looking for is there all along. The *feeling* of abundance which you so eagerly yearn for has been there waiting for you all along to experience it.

Why does the mind search for so many answers on the outside? It searches for answers to keep you safe. It believes that without the answers, you will suffer unwanted outcomes. Therefore, it keeps projecting these endless disaster and worst-case scenarios in your mind in an attempt to keep you safe. This is where so much of our mind chatter comes from. All our mind chatter is not real; it is merely our old ways of responding to stuff as we have always done. If your mind has only known financial lack all its life, then that is the only picture it can paint if left to itself. Similarly, if your mind has known financial abundance all its life, then the picture of abundance is the only picture it knows how to project continually onto the world. The good news is that you can change this picture in your mind, anytime and at will. It is *just* a picture in your mind.

What I am suggesting here goes beyond all that. Remember how I told you we are not trying to make anything happen in this book? Remember what I said about not trying to go anywhere or even seek the right answers? That's why I invite you not even to try and "paint" any pictures in your mind. Don't force a picture of abundance in your mind. That may be difficult for some people. To a mind that has always defaulted to pictures of lack, it can be challenging to deliberately conjure up images of prosperity. Hence, give all of that up. Don't even try to do it. All I suggest is that you close your eyes, clear all thoughts from your mind and gently hold the intention of *abundance*. What does abundance feel like to you?

For me, abundance feels like ease and flow. It feels like safety and security. It feels like something solid and dependable that I can use for support in my life. That is the *feeling* of abundance for me. Close your eyes right now and get in touch with your feelings of abundance. If you had all the money you desired, how would it feel like to you? Your feelings will be unique to you, and they may have a certain intangible quality to them. You may not be able to easily describe the resulting feeling in words, but you'll always know it when you feel it. It will feel special and just right for you.

Don't even try to describe your feeling of abundance in words. We limit ourselves the moment we try to put words and labels to our experience. Instead, focus on the full experiencing of the abundant feeling. You may feel a general sense of lightness and joy, or an incredible sense of freedom. Whatever the feelings are, immerse yourself in them.

In the beginning, you may not be able to "feel" your full abundance. You may feel just a little bit of it, but it is there all the same. This is alright because we have all been so conditioned to pay attention to what goes on outside of ourselves that we have forgotten how to use our inner senses. We have lost touch with our inner world. But our inner world will *always be there*. Therefore don't be afraid that you have to seek hard for it, otherwise, it will disappear. It will not disappear. Those feelings of inner abundance are always there for your discovery, no matter when you return to them. They are a part of the eternal essence of who you are, and not some fleeting illusion.

As such, know that even if you do not manage to connect with the full essence of this abundance in a single sitting, it does not mean these feelings are not there. Right now, you are standing in a beautiful field of flowers. This is a wonderful analogy to use and a wonderful imagery to remind yourself of. Take a photo (or find a beautiful picture) of a field of your favorite flowers, one that shows blooming flowers stretching out all the way into the horizon. If you need some reminder of this timeless spiritual truth, take a look at the photo. No words are necessary. The imagery will remind you that you are *already* immersed in your field of goodness.

CHAPTER THREE

HOW TO USE YOUR ALWAYS-ON CONNECTION TO THE UNIVERSE

You can be standing in the most magnificent field of flowers but still be missing the magnificence and beauty of it all if your focus is somewhere else. For most of us, our focus is naturally misplaced. It is constantly occupied and taken up by the issues and problems we perceive in our lives. So many of us are far too busy putting out one fire after the next, dealing with one petty concern after the next that we hardly take the time to notice where we are standing. If we only took the time to look inward, we would immediately recognize the abundance that has always been there.

My intention for you as you read this book is to completely place all your money "issues" and perceived "problems" out of your mind, at least during the time we spend together. Take all of that out of the equation. Don't even spend a single moment dwelling on it. Understand that you do not have to look at reality unless it pleases you because even the "reality" you are going through now is the old reality. It is already in the past, and a new reality is in the process of *becoming*. Understand that in each moment of your life, energy is always flowing and things are always going into form and out of form. When you become fixated by the physical "form" of things, by what things have become *in the moment*, you allow yourself to be taken in by the illusion of that form. When you fixate on your bank balance, or on how much money you have at the moment, you allow yourself to *believe* that it is the whole, unchanging reality. But it is not the whole reality. It is your *old* reality which is in the process of becoming something *else*. What that something else is depends on <u>you</u> and your new focus.

The good news is that you don't have to be thinking about money all the time to manifest more of it into your life. You don't have to be thinking about financial abundance or prosperity all the time to have it in your life. You can think about any of the thousands of subjects that feel *similar* in vibration to the subject of wealth, prosperity, and abundance. This means you can just as easily think about something that feels good for you, and money will flow easily into your experience as you relax.

This frees up a lot of the burden for most people because it means that they no longer need to fuss over the small details of their lives. You no longer need to repeat affirmations or engage yourself in continued detailed visualizations. Of course, you can still continue to engage in them if they make you feel so happy and good, but it is just as alright if you choose to skip them. Know that <u>your good will still flow to you</u> even if you did not do any of the minute "planning" or asking. If you left everything up to the Universe and dropped your feelings of worry and fear...everything good will still happen for you, in a way that pleases and delights you.

The ego thinks that it has to do all sorts of "planning" to make things happen. As such, it plans and conceives of even the smallest details. Then the ego convinces us that we have to keep visualizing, keep affirming, or keep holding a mental picture in our minds such that this mental picture will be brought to fruition. This causes much of the stress and dissonance in most people. They are worried that if they lapse in their practice of "picturing their good" for even one single moment that things will not happen for them. Give all of these faulty and mistaken beliefs up! Your good is <u>not dependent</u> on anything that you DO. Your good is <u>not dependent</u> on you constantly picturing it in your mind. Your good is not even up to you because it is already here. It exists in the here and now. Any mental picture that you strain to hold only creates unnecessary stress and tension in your body system.

Picture yourself amongst a beautiful field of flowers. You are here now. The flowers stretch in all directions, as far as your eyes can see. But what if you wrongly believed that you have to picture every single flower in your mind in great vivid detail before they can be there? They would still be there nonetheless, but your mind would be elsewhere. Your mind would be preoccupied with conjuring up an accurate mental picture and ensuring that you "get it right." All your enjoyment would be taken away from you. You have just gone from heaven-on-earth to hell-on-earth. You are still physically in the same place amongst those beautiful flowers, but a simple shift of perception has caused the enjoyment of your good to be greatly affected.

So don't make this mistake for even a moment longer. Turn your focus inwards and recognize the beautiful field of flowers, the infinite abundance that already lies within. This is going to be difficult to do in the beginning, especially if you have adopted an outward focus for your entire life. Most people have learned to judge themselves based on their bank balances for their entire lives. They have allowed their net worth to determine their self-worth. This is why modern society and popular culture reveres the rich so much. They have become living gods on a pedestal. But aren't these individuals the same as the rest of us? We are all made of the same mind stuff. We have exactly the same tools as these individuals, and therefore, there is nothing they have done that we cannot do if you hold similar intentions.

Stop judging yourself based on how much money you have, how much money you earn, or how much debt you hold. All of these are already in the past. They are part of your old reality. In this very moment, they are changing into something else. What do you want them to change into? Would you want them to change into more of the same...or into a reality that will please and delight you wholeheartedly? If you choose the latter, then you must begin to exercise your focus in a completely new way.

By exercising your focus, I do not mean conjuring up detailed mental images of your good. I do not mean going to great lengths to picture yourself in abundance. That is not the mental focus I am referring to here. Instead, all I am referring to is what you place your *awareness* on in this moment. Individuals who are worried about money often place their constant awareness on the fact that they do not have enough. They rest their focus there and constantly worry about fluctuations in their bank account. Or they place their awareness on their debt and constantly remind themselves about how much debt they have. If only they would withdraw that awareness and place it *somewhere else*, they would experience the most glorious flow of abundance they have ever known in their lives! That is all it takes.

Right now, you are placing your gentle awareness on my words. This in itself is a huge step forward because your awareness is no longer on things that stress you. You can also exercise this ability to mentally focus even further and place it on the feelings of abundance you feel on the inside. The exercise we did in Chapter 2 was to have you place your mental awareness on those inner feelings of abundance. The more you do it and the more you allow your awareness to remain there...the more changes you will observe in your outer circumstances. Remember that all of these happen *even without you lifting a finger.* Your job is not to do any of the menial physical work. I say this not because we are lazy or because we shun away from physical work, but because until we achieve mental clarity on the inside...any physical work that we do will be minuscule compared to what can be done by the Universe through us. Our physical efforts, if not aligned with the flow of the Universe, is like a single drop in the vast ocean.

Return to these inner feelings of abundance you have on the inside for as much of your day as possible. You'll find that as you place your mental awareness there over-and-over again, you'll be able to feel these feelings intensify over time. This does not mean that your abundance has grown. It is impossible for something that is already infinite to grow. Rather, it simply means that you are becoming more and more aware of your greater good. You are coming into greater recognition of the infinite good and potential that is already within you. You are placing more emphasis on your inner state rather than the outer world. These will be the first signs of progress.

You will have intrusive thoughts as you try all of the above. This is expected. In the beginning, these intrusive thoughts (stemming from your ego and faulty conditioning) will let you know that you are wasting your time, or that you are escaping from the problems which need to be "solved" in the real world. But ironically, what the ego knows is also wrong. The ego attempts to solve the problem by presenting various practical solutions, but its solutions are often misplaced and misguided. Its belief that there are problems in the first place is misguided. If there are no problems or issues in the first place, then what needs to be solved or resolved? All is well, and there is nothing that needs to be "corrected" in your life. The only thing that needs correction or gentle guidance is <u>where you place your conscious awareness on most of the time</u>.

Does it seem magical to you that our outer reality automatically fills itself up without any input from us? Does it seem implausible that the Universe already knows our deepest desires and preferences? Once you understand how these great Universal Laws work, none of it will seem strange to you any longer. In fact, it will all become quite natural. The Universe is always picking up on the sum total of our thoughts and feelings *all of the time*. It has an impeccable receiving and recording mechanism. Every thought or intention we've had, no matter how small or slight, makes an impression in the Universal fabric.

This is the reason why there is no need to hold detailed pictures in our mind or go into great details about what we want. This will only tire ourselves out needlessly. The Universe has already picked up on our billions of small intentions and preferences each time we had them, even though we were not consciously visualizing or affirming at that time! In the moment we allow our good to come to us (by completely withdrawing our focus from negative feelings and the perceived issues in our lives)…all of these preferences and desires are delivered to us in one fell swoop. But it is not magic, we have simply forgotten that we even asked for certain things at earlier points in our lives.

The Universe will reveal its inner workings and intricacies to you if you look closely at your life. I am in awe of the magic and miracles that are there when I simply pay attention and notice.

Suppose that you step into a meeting room and notice that the temperature is too cold. In that moment, without even realizing it, you have just set an intention for the temperature of the room to be more comfortable. This intention is picked up and held perfectly by the Universe. Then you take a seat and notice that the chair is too high. Again, an implicit, unspoken intention for the chair to be of the right height is picked up by the Universe. You then notice that you are seated right where you are, in your favorite spot of the room. That intention again, this time a positive preference, is picked up perfectly by the Universe. As you set your foot down on the carpet, you appreciate how lush the carpeting is and how luxurious the meeting room looks. Again, all of these preferences are picked up and held perfectly by the Universe.

Take a look at how many intentions we have set in the short span of a few minutes. It is the same for you and me in every moment of our life. As I am writing this book, I appreciate the comfortable temperature of my room. I am appreciating the huge and wide screen that allows me to view what I have written without straining my eyes. All of these preferences are picked up upon and held perfectly by the Universe. In the moment that we *allow* our good to come to us, all of these preferences are then delivered back to us in the most appropriate ways. You may step into that meeting room the next time round and find that "by chance," the temperature is now just right for you. You may also find that "by chance," the seat is at the right position without you having to adjust it.

But all these did not just happen "by chance", all of them fell into place because your intentions and preferences gave rise to these desires at earlier points in your life. It may be from the past minute, the past hour, the past week, month or even decade...but once you have unconsciously set an intention, it is always held in perfect harmony until you change it in some way.

The same applies to your financial situation as well. Each time you looked at your finances, you were setting unconscious intentions that were picked up perfectly by the Universe. Each time you looked at your bank balance and appreciated (or hated) it, you were setting intentions for more of the same. And therefore, there is no need for us to even worry about whether we are "doing things right" when it comes to setting intentions and manifestations. How can we be doing things wrong when in each moment, the Universe is picking up on the sum total of our thoughts and feelings perfectly, even right down to the smallest details?

When you realize that you have this constant connection to the Universe, you understand your sacred place amongst that field of beautiful flowers and how all this relates to your physical manifestations.

Chapter Four

The Truth Shall Set You Free (And It's Not What You Think)

Isn't it ironic that in a book focused on money, we have discussed very little about the specifics of money and your financial situation? This is, of course, deliberate.

The first ten years of my spiritual journey were filled with pain and anguish, not because the Universe was not responding to my requests but because I spent more than half the time immersed in my self-created problems and then tried to get out of them. It may be hard for you to grasp this spiritual truth all at once, but stick with me for just a bit longer and everything will become clear—Our continued fixation on a perceived problem *perpetuates* the problem, long after the original cause is gone. The same applies to any financial blockage or lack which you perceive in your life. The lack is there because of your continued focus and perception of it. If you take your mind (and eyes) away from the lack for a sufficiently long period of time, things will sort themselves out in an instant. This is Universal Law.

But how does one begin? How do you even begin to take your eyes (or mind) off something that you perceive to be so important for your well-being? Doing so would be irresponsible, or at least that is what society has attempted to teach us. Society has taught us to be practical, to always keep an eye on our problems so that we can solve them. But if this way of problem-solving works, there would not be any problems remaining. We would all solve our problems and be done with them. Everywhere we turn, people are complaining about the stressful recurring problems and issues in their lives. When one issue is settled, another one is waiting for them around the corner. So what's the root cause here? The cause is our <u>continued fixation on the perceived issues of our life</u>.

The situation can be tricky when it comes to our finances. Since such a large part of our well-being is tied to our finances, it is easy to be reminded of our financial situation whenever we make buying decisions or pay our bills. Most of us compound the issue without realizing it. Let me explain. Suppose that you perceive "financial lack" in your life right now, and you think you do not have enough money. Your bank balance is always a concern to you, and you are frequently worried about how much money you have in the bank, whether you can pay the bills when they are due and whether you'll have enough money for your expenses.

What do you suppose is the real issue here? The fact that your bank balance is low, or your continued and sustained worry over the state of your bank balance? Think carefully before giving an answer, because this answer will give you the epiphany that you need. For the first ten years of my spiritual journey, I used to think that the former was the real issue. I used to think that the *fact* that my bank balance was low was the objective reality. That was the reality I was perpetuating at that time. What I did not realize is that the latter was actually the true cause of the perceived financial lack in my life: It was my continued and sustained worries over my bank balance that kept perpetuating the low bank balance, not the other way round.

This is a leap in thinking that most people struggle to make. But once you successfully make it, this simple switch can be the most liberating thing in the world for you. The truth will set you free! In other words, if you are worrying sixteen hours a day about money, then your sixteen hours of worrying is the true root cause of the problem, <u>not</u> the external financial situation. You are spending sixteen hours immersed in an unwanted, undesirable inner state which will subsequently lead to outer manifestations! The low bank balance by itself <u>is not the problem</u> because it is just one version of reality which can be changed. It is *old* reality caused by your old thinking, and thus can be replaced by something better from this point forward.

When I introduce this idea to people, they are amazed by how easy it is to change their reality. Naturally, they are also skeptical since they have spent most of their lives worrying! But here's a way which will allow you to step into a new reality very quickly: Instead of worrying endlessly about your finances and debt, make a conscious decision right now to worry about them for just 15 minutes a day. That's right. Set aside 15 minutes a day, where you can just sit quietly by yourself and worry all you want about your problems. However, after those 15 minutes are up, tell yourself that you are done with your worrying for the day. All your worrying should be done within that allotted time for the day, and any "new" worrying should be done during the next day!

Do you see what we have just done here and how powerful this technique is? We have just gone from sixteen waking hours of worrying to just fifteen minutes a day. And if you can go from sixteen hours down to fifteen minutes, you'll be able to go from fifteen to just five minutes...and eventually to none. But I do not expect anyone to make the leap from a lifetime of worrying to giving up their habit instantly. This method of creating a special "worry time" for yourself will help as it drastically reduces the amount of time in which you spend negatively creating.

One common objection I receive is this: "But if I just ignore my problems, they do not go away! This is a form of escape!" To the ego mind, this *seems* like a form of escape. It seems as if you are dodging the problems in your life instead of facing them head-on. But let's be realistic for a moment: Sum up all the time you spent "worrying" about your finances in the past day, week, month, or year. You'll be surprised at the amount of time you have been stewing in these negative, worrisome thoughts! Has this brought about an improvement of the situation? Has this led to a more desired reality? Maybe it is time to try something different since this method has not worked despite the amount of time we have put in.

If you succeed in going from sixteen hours of worrying right down to sixteen minutes of worrying per day, things will change in an instant for you. All of a sudden, good things will start happening in your outer reality for you. This is not just mere "fantasy"—I have lived it, and so have thousands of readers around the world who have taken the time to write heartfelt reviews for my books. They certainly did not have to do so, and I never ask for reviews for my books. All that I ask for is that you *give these techniques a chance.* Try them. Try this new way of thinking and acting in the world. You have nothing to lose and everything to gain. Even if my method of reducing your worry time does not work and does absolutely nothing to your finances, you would still emerge a much happier person. That would be a drastic improvement from the way which most people are living now.

Let me share how things turned around very quickly for me once I began to apply the principles in this chapter. Hopefully, you too can take a leaf out of my book. For the first ten years of my spiritual journey, I was constantly worried about not having enough money. My "low" bank balance was the root cause of the problem to me, and I attempted to use all sorts of metaphysical techniques and methods to "improve" my financial situation. Because I was so fixated on the issue, I spent most of my waking hours thinking (and worrying) about my financial situation. It was like a sick feeling in my gut I could not get rid of. Along with worrying came a whole host of negative emotions, such as blame, guilt, sadness and self-criticism. Understand that all of this is merely the Law of Attraction at work. The Law of Attraction was working round-the-clock to bring me more negative feelings that *matched* the worrying feelings I already held all day.

How did I arrive at the sixteen-hour figure in the previous example? It was from my own life. I spent almost sixteen hours a day worrying about money and all the things that could go wrong in my life as a result of not having enough money. The only time I did not worry was when I was asleep, or when I was engrossed in some form of focused activity or entertainment. Still, when left to its own devices, my brain automatically defaulted to worrying and fear thoughts. I never perceived my continued worrying as *the* issue, which is why I never tackled it head-on. I kept thinking that my low bank balance was the issue and cause of everything, which is why I tried so hard to overcome it through my use of various convoluted metaphysical techniques. Understand that the physical situation which you perceive to be the "problem" is never the problem, because any situation in outer physical reality is the result of your inner state. Return your inner state to one of peace, and the outer circumstances will straighten themselves out.

During that period of my life, I frequently drove past a church which had the words "THE TRUTH SHALL SET YOU FREE" printed in big, bold letters. I remember reading those words and feeling a deep connection to them on the inside without really knowing why. Perhaps it was the Universe's way of telling me that everything I needed, the truth that I so desperately sought was already inside of me... and when I *realized* it, I would finally be free. True enough, the "truth" that I needed was indeed inside of me...and once I saw my negative worry feelings as the true cause of my problems, everything corrected themselves within a short time.

Let's talk about dealing with the more practical aspects. Suppose that your bank balance worries you, and you know that it is a tangible part of your current reality. How do you ignore it or stop worrying about it so much? The way I did it was simply to not take a look or pay any attention to it unless I absolutely needed to. This means that I went from thinking about my bank balance almost every other moment, to thinking about it only once or twice a month when I needed to pay my bills. This simple switch in behavior helped immensely because it reduced a lot of the associated worries and anxieties that I had. So make some lifestyle changes to avoid bringing up those worry feelings. Remember it is the *feelings you frequently hold* that are the issue, not the unwanted manifestation itself.

Take a look at your life and identify certain activities that frequently make you anxious or worried. For some people, it can be the simple act of paying for something with their credit card. If the mere act of *using* your credit card reminds you about your debt and makes you feel worried about whether you can pay your bill when it arrives...stop using your card! Find creative ways to work around these activities. For example, you can change your lifestyle habits such that you pay for most of your purchases in cash. Withdraw some cash from the bank at the start of the month and pay cash for your purchases during the month. This simple switch may not eliminate your debt overnight, but what it will do is to change the way you feel about your debt. This simple move reduces the number of times you are reminded of your financial situation during the day, and it can go a long way in terms of your physical manifestations.

How many times do you worry about your bank balance or the amount of money you have within a day? How about reducing that number to zero? That would not only make a huge difference in the way you feel; it would also make a tremendous difference to your outer reality as it relates to money. Once I switched to this new way of thinking and acting in the world, my previously perceived problems with my financial situation simply fell away. Everything dissolved on its own accord within a few months. Suddenly, new sources of income and business opened up for me. The money came to me from all the different sources that delighted me. When I needed to buy something or fulfill a need, the money was already there for me. I did not even have to start the process of asking for it.

But is it magic? Not at all. It all started with making one simple change in my life—that of recognizing that what I previously believed to be the ultimate "truth" and ultimate "reality" was not my reality at all. All that was merely an illusion perpetuated by my own inner state. Once I restored my inner state back to its natural place of love and peace, everything else good on the outside followed.

Chapter Five

Nothing You Desire is Ever Out of Your League

The very good news is that none of this work is predicated on your personal belief. You may not *believe* that dollars can flow to you easily, but they would still do if you put yourself in a position to receive your Universal good. You may not *believe* that you can turn your financial situation around at all, but it would still change for the better if you acted in accordance with these Universal Laws. You may not believe that changes can be made in a very short time, but time is of no relevance to the Universe. Therefore, rest in the assurance that your current level of <u>belief</u> plays a very small part in your manifestations. Instead, what matters the most is where you <u>choose</u> to place your continued focus on despite your beliefs.

Let me explain. When I asked for some really big things in my life, I did not really believe that I could achieve them. In fact, I was skeptical most of the time! None of my friends around me had achieved the same results I was asking for, and no one from my family or social circle had dared to ask for similar things. As such, I was operating under the mistaken belief that those good things were not supposed to be mine. They were out of my league! I am thankful that the Universe does not work in this manner. Despite my disbelief that I could have whatever I asked for, physical manifestations still happened for me. All that is needed on your part is a *willingness* to focus on the desired end result and <u>stay there long enough</u> until things happen on the outside. That is the only work you need to do. Leave everything else to the Universe.

If we had to *truly* believe in something before the Universe could give it to us, many of our manifestations would still be unfulfilled. Since most people have trouble manifesting their deepest desires, they wrongly think that it is because they do not "believe" that they can have what they ask for. They ascribe their lack of physical manifestations to their lack of belief.

A lack of physical belief has never caused anyone's manifestations to be withheld from them. However, if one's lack of belief translates into corresponding feelings of worry, disappointment, resentment or failure...then those feelings are going to be picked up by the Universe, and that is going to be what is manifested. In other words, while the lack of belief alone is not fatal to our manifestations, the corresponding negative emotions caused by our lack of belief can be an impediment to our manifestations.

Once you understand this principle, you immediately free yourself from the need to do any of the "belief" work. Let's suppose that you want to create a reality in which dollars flow to you easily. Before you understood this principle, you might have spent lots of time visualizing and "feeling the feelings" of dollars flowing to you easily, in the hope that such a scenario will be more "believable" to you. Or you may have continually pictured yourself living your life with a higher level of income until that mental picture felt "real" to you. Give up the need to make anything "real" or "believable" to you. As we have already established, your level of belief plays a very small role in your physical manifestations. What matters is whether you hold emotions and feelings that are *in accordance with* and in line with what you are asking for.

Suppose that you are asking for more abundance in your life. You are asking for a greater flow of money and dollars into your life. You do not have to <u>believe</u> that it is possible for you to live this way, so take belief out of the equation. What you instead have to do is to *stop focusing on* the "lack" in your current situation. This means to stop feeling those feelings of worry, fear, disappointment and blame associated with your financial situation. This also means to stop stewing over them for most of your day. If you'll take this simple step of reducing your time spent worrying, then your good comes automatically into your life <u>whether you believe in it or</u>

<u>not</u>. In fact, you can *believe* very strongly that you will be rich (through immense and intense visualizations) or long periods of mental conditioning…but until you let go of those negative feelings of worry and fear, what you believe in can never come to you.

Once you achieve this level of understanding, you are instantly liberated to create even better and greater things. Things that up till now have seemed impossible or out of your league. Nothing is ever out of your league, but they can be out of the league of your *feelings* and *inner state*. If you intend abundance and prosperity on one hand but spend your days mired in worry and fear, then you are keeping yourself apart from what you have asked for. You are allowing yourself to manifest the exact opposite of what you have asked for.

When I first began focusing on my inner state and returning it to that natural place of love and peace, my physical reality still stayed the same for a while. For a few weeks, my bank balance still remained the same. The more I looked at my bank balance (physical reality) on the outside, the more I was convinced that things would not work out for me. Therefore, a part of myself was still skeptical that things would not happen, and that it would still be the same old results all over again.

However, what was different this time was that I did not allow myself to dwell on those feelings of disappointment or worry for long. I knew better. I knew that while my physical reality still *seemed* the same on the outside, powerful changes were happening on the inside. Each time I saw my bank balance or came into mental contact with it for whatever reason, I would mentally remind myself that things were changing on the inside and that this change would soon be reflected in my outer reality.

True enough, within the next few weeks, physical evidence began to occur for me on the outside. I began receiving checks in the mail and business opportunities which I had not actively solicited. People and events were now coming to me and falling into my lap without my active intervention or input. This is the Universe working its magic and bringing you the things that are <u>in line with</u> your <u>predominant</u> inner state. If you hold that inner state of highest love and peace such that *nothing* on the outside can disturb you, then soon nothing on the outside will disturb you. Everything that you draw to yourself will bring more joy and happiness into your life. But you must make the change on the inside first.

This is why I keep harping on the need to ignore physical reality for the time being. Physical reality is not even solid. It is not everlasting or permanent. It is merely a reflection, a mirror of our inner states. Physical reality can be changed in an instant just like this! We have been conditioned all our lives to believe in how *real* everything on the outside is, not realizing that this reality can be changed at any time simply by working with the very forces that create our Universe. Therefore, no matter how your physical situation looks like at the moment, pay no

ง

Richard Dotts

attention to it unless it pleases you. Instead, turn your full attention to the way you feel on the inside. Do you feel good most of the time? Do you feel at peace most of the time? Or do you worry most of the time about the bad things that can happen to you? I can assure you that your inner state mirrors your outer reality perfectly. If you have a peaceful inner state, your outer reality will be beautiful and perfect. If you have a tumultuous inner state, your outer reality will be equally chaotic.

When you recognize this link between the way you feel on the inside and your manifested reality on the outside, you would have stumbled upon a very importance piece of the manifestation puzzle. Manifestations are not about *trying* to make something happen on the outside. You are not trying to "attract" money, or anything good into your life as if you are a magnet. Instead, you are opening your eyes to the abundance and the natural flow that is already there for your picking. The prosperity has been there all along, but you have not been able to receive or enjoy it. Why is that so? You have not been able to enjoy it *not* because you were undeserving of all that good or because of your sins, but because you were focused somewhere else. You were (through the power of your own thoughts and imagination) focused on a reality where there was lack and limitation, and therefore continually perpetuating lack and limitation.

Right now, you may perceive things as being at a dead end. You may not see the light at the end of the

44

tunnel. It seems like you're in an endless tunnel with no way out. But know that everything is only energy and that the physical reality which you currently perceive as being stuck is also made up of energy. It is held in place *by* energy, which is always flowing and always in motion. What you perceive as a stuck situation is merely energy reorganizing and reforming itself into the same thing over and over again.

If I wanted to project the same image onto a movie screen for one minute, the film spool would still have to keep advancing during that minute. What has to be done is to copy the same image and repeat it several times across all the frames shown during that minute. This is a wonderful analogy because what we perceive to be "static" and unchanging on the big screen are new frames being repeated over-and-over again. Our senses *think* we are looking at the same thing, but the underlying frames used to project that image are changing every single moment. Strictly speaking, we are looking at a new *image* with every new frame, just that it is an image of the same thing over-and-over again.

This projector analogy illustrates the nature of our thoughts and feelings. Whatever is in your inner state is whatever goes on each frame. Whatever is projected onto the big screen is your outer, manifested reality. You just have to change the picture on the small frame to change whatever is projected on the big screen. The problem is that over time, we have come to believe that the projected image on the big screen is real because it is so big and vivid!

It occupies all of our attention. We've forgotten that the outer image can easily be changed by simply imprinting a new image on the frame!

If you don't like what is in your current physical reality, always remind yourself that you are dealing with an outer projection that is put in place (and perpetuated by) your inner states. Therefore, don't curse whatever is on the screen, make a conscious decision to change it from the inside! Start by changing your inner state this very moment. Restore it to one of ease and peace, free from any worries, struggle or strain. Your external circumstances will soon match up to this new mental frame that you have created.

Chapter Six

How to Manifest Money and Abundance in Your Life

If you skipped straight to this chapter because of its fancy title, I would advise you to read this book right from the beginning. Without the firm spiritual grounding and foundation laid by the rest of this book, you will not benefit from the full power of the spiritual exercises outlined in this chapter, neither will you understand their true significance.

Over the years, I have tried literally thousands of techniques to attract money and wealth into my life. These techniques range from the downright esoteric to bizarre, some of which I am even embarrassed to name here! We all know how we can sometimes be driven to the edge in desperation...when we desperately *want* something to work and are willing to try anything, at any cost.

Fortunately for me, the search ended once I realized these Universal Principles. I am first going to lay down a few counter-intuitive spiritual principles before going through them in greater detail. The single biggest reason why people try endless metaphysical techniques to manifest what they want is because they perceive a *lack* of the things they are asking for. In other words, we try to attract money into our lives because we perceive money as lacking. Sounds simple enough, doesn't it? But there is also a deeper spiritual significance.

What if I told you that money isn't really lacking in your life? If someone had told me this back then, I might have thought they were crazy! Every single physical sign pointed to the money *not* being in my life...and here is a guy who tells me that money isn't really lacking in my life? What if I kick it up a notch and tell you that not only is money not *lacking* in your life, it is actually present in great quantities and great abundance right now. Are you still with me?

Look, I am not referring to metaphors commonly used by motivational authors. I am not saying that there is a great amount of wealth and abundance in the world right now, and there is more than enough for everyone. What I am saying is that *in your life this very moment,* there is an endless flow of wealth, prosperity, and abundance. Right now, you are standing amongst a field of beautiful flowers without even realizing it. You are in your own field of goodness without even realizing that you are there. Therefore, how can you ask for *more* abundance or money to come into your life...when you already have everything you need? How can you ask for *more* to be added to *more?*

Give up the notion that you need to ask for money in your life. All the money you need is already here for your taking and usage. But why don't you see it yet? Why isn't this truth reflected in your bank accounts yet? The reason is that you are asking for the money so hard, that is what you are resonating with every single moment of your day. Your feelings of lack and worry are so *strong* that it is where your entire consciousness is focused. If you can find a way right now, this very moment, to <u>reduce your feelings of lack down to zero</u>, to be in a place of nothingness and a state of no worries...then all the money you need will flow into your physical experience quicker than you can imagine.

Therefore, *asking* hard for something is a large part of the "problem." When you perceive a need to *ask very hard* and *desperately* for something, you are confirming its lack in your life. That's why you need to ask so hard for it...because the thing which you seek is not here yet! And if you continue to immerse yourself in these feelings of lack and not-here-yet, then that is the reality which you are going to perpetuate. Reality (and the underlying energy) is constantly changing and flowing every single moment, just that you have (through the power of your own thoughts) forced reality to change into the same unwanted circumstances over and over again.

What was the technique I used that allowed me to overcome the tides of my own negative feelings and conditioning? It is simple. I simply disconnected myself from all my negative, worrying and lackful thoughts. I closed my eyes and focused within. I stopped asking for money in my life. I just closed my eyes, went within and became still. Not expecting anything, not wanting anything, and not wanting to make anything happen.

When you have been immersed in lackful and negative thoughts surrounding money for the longest time, the first thing you have to do is to disconnect yourself from all those negatively creative thoughts. Disconnect from them completely by not even trying to replace them with something positive. Instead, go into the void where there is only emptiness and <u>stay there</u>. Disconnect from all of your past fears, worries and all that negative messy thinking about your financial situation. Don't even think about it! Go into your inner world and immerse yourself in the emptiness there.

When you first attempt to do this exercise, a few things may result. In the first couple of minutes, all the worry and fear thoughts are still going to pass through your conscious awareness and grip you. They are still going to appear in all forms and scare you. But each time those thoughts appear, understand that they are merely projections of your ego. They are not real. They can be changed. But don't even try to change them. Instead, just notice them and let the thoughts gently drift past. Don't follow the stream of thoughts and entertain a single thought in your own mind. Just breathe deeply and focus within.

After the first couple of minutes have passed, you may find the intensity of these worrisome thoughts decreasing. You may notice an underlying good feeling, like goosebumps welling up all over your body and a sense of unconditional well-being. Notice how this good feeling is not conditional on anything that is in your external reality. It arises spontaneously. This is part of your true spiritual essence. It is your natural state. This good feeling is always there, whether you are aware of it or not. This good feeling is your first recognition of the glorious abundance that lies within. You are starting to notice these good feelings that have always been there.

As you start to pay attention to these good feelings, they will intensify in a way that is profound and personal for you. You may feel spontaneous feelings of joy, peace, and excitement on the inside. I can feel this feeling even as I am writing these words. I can feel the underlying sense of great peace and joy just welling up underneath the surface of my conscious awareness. This is the infinite power that we all have access to. This is our eternal essence and our eternal abundance. Notice also, that when you pay attention to these underlying good feelings that you feel further and further away from your fear and worry thoughts. The more you notice these good feelings within yourself, the less you notice or think those negative fear thoughts. Those negative fear thoughts simply cannot exist when you are aware of the good feelings.

What is happening here? When we are aware of the underlying pleasant feelings that we have beneath our conscious awareness, we are opening our inner eyes to the field of flowers (abundance) that has always been there. We are recognizing this great spiritual truth, and coming face-to-face with it possibly for the first time. Notice how *no effort* is needed on your part to feel these good and pleasant feelings. No work is needed on your part. **You do not have to *try* and feel good, or *try and conjure* up these good feelings**. There is no trying. There is no doing. There is only being. Right now in this very moment, there is only *beingness*. You are not even engaged in any action to make something happen. Simply by becoming still, quieting the mind from your usual thoughts and dropping those extraneous thoughts from your mind...you are coming *face to face* with your true and abundant nature.

I want you to observe and notice how *no work is required at all on your part* to feel these good feelings. Observe how this no-work feeling feels like. Observe how this feeling of non-action and no-doing feels like. You are not *doing* anything. You are just sitting there quietly in your chair and *perceiving* these good feelings. You are perceiving Universal Goodness simply by slowly becoming aware of it.

This is the only proof you need that Universal Goodness, and universal abundance exists for every single one of us. This is, in fact, the **surest proof** that it exists! I have never tried hard to convince anyone in words that our Universal Good flows for each and every one of us. Instead, I have always invited them to try this powerful exercise for themselves. When you quieten the mind and focus within, you notice those spontaneous good feelings welling up within you without any effort on your part. The fact that spontaneous good feelings well up with no intervention or input on your part means they are your natural birthright. This is a natural phenomenon. This happens whether you like it or not. Your good flows to you whether you are aware of it or not, whether you ask for it or not, whether you *think* you deserve it or not.

This experiment proves to us clearly that our good flows to us on its own accord! There is an unlimited supply of benevolent, Universal energy that is always flowing to us. If the Universe is not benevolent in nature (as some people falsely believe), if we had to struggle hard for our good (as many people wrongly believe), then you would feel absolutely *nothing* or even *bad feelings* as you did this exercise. You would not be able to perceive anything "good" coming to you. These pleasant feelings would not become apparent to you.

Why is it that millions of individuals around the world who have tried this exercise in one form or another felt only *goodness* flowing to them? Why is it that millions of individuals who are so different in their beliefs, education, culture, upbringing or lifestyle...have felt (or will feel) the Universal Goodness flowing to them **the moment** they do this exercise, with absolutely no effort on their part?

Notice what happened in your case. What did you have to do to perceive this Universal Goodness? That's right; you had to *do* absolutely nothing! There was nothing you needed to do, no place you needed to go, no action you needed to take. Instead, you only had to *drop* certain thoughts from your conscious awareness. You had to *drop* the negative and fear thoughts that were competing for your conscious awareness and attention that same moment. You had to momentarily pay no attention to them before you could perceive the underlying goodness that has always been there. You had to take off your tinted glasses to see the world as the Universe sees it.

Do you realize now why this is the best "technique" I have used for manifesting wealth and abundance in my life? This is not even a "technique" because there is nothing to do. All I did was to merely sit quietly by myself in a place where I would not be interrupted, close my eyes and focus inwards. Once I had done so, I observed the mind chatter that went by without engaging in any of it. Gradually, I perceived the Universal Goodness (or *Magic Feeling* as I describe in my book of the same name) until my perception of these pleasant feelings became more and more intense. That is the only thing you have to *do,* if you have to do anything at all. Three times a day of fifteen minutes each will disconnect and disengage you from your old reality and create a new opening that is just what is needed for wealth and abundance to flow into your life.

Chapter Seven

Your Universal Secretary Keeps Perfect Records

Some people who read the technique in the previous chapter will immediately see the light. They will immediately understand the value of disconnecting and disengaging from their negative thoughts, which have never been true anyway. They will understand the power of going into the void, the field of infinite possibilities and letting the Universe do its magic. Yet I know that for every reader who understands this logic, there will be others who will ask this exact question, "How does the Universe know what I want if I just sit there without verbalizing my desires or visualizing them? How does the Universe know the amount of money I need or what I am asking for?"

This is a great question as it ties in beautifully with what we have discussed so far. Recall how I mentioned that the Universe is always picking up on your deepest desires and preferences, no matter how small they are? Recall how the simple act of setting foot into a meeting room and sitting down on a chair triggered a whole series of intentions, desires, and preferences which were then picked up by the Universe? Therefore, understand and rest in the assurance that you have done *enough asking* in the past. Whether you realize it or not, the Universe had picked up (and is constantly picking up) on your deepest intentions and desires, even when you did not think the Universe was listening.

Each time you saw a nice car drive past and said to yourself, "Wow that's a nice car!", you were signaling your desire and intention for similar cars <u>without even having to consciously set an intention for it!</u> Each time you drove past a nice house in a nice neighborhood and appreciated all the beautiful things about it, you were signaling your intention and desire to the Universe to <u>draw similar things into your life</u>. Without realizing it, you have put all sorts of wonderful good things into your wish list... more so than you can ever imagine.

This is like having a meticulous secretary always by your side, taking care of your every single whim and fancy. Each time you expressed a liking or dislike for something, the Universal secretary noted it down in her notebook perfectly. (Well, she must be using a very thick notebook indeed!) But don't worry about how the Universe stores any of that, the Universe has the means to store all of your intentions and desires perfectly.

Here's the interesting thing about this Universal secretary that is always by your side: Apart from having a very thick notebook (or several of them), she can't tell the difference between your likes and dislikes! In other words, when you saw a beautiful red car and said, "I would love to have a car like that!", the Universal secretary made an entry titled "red car" into your notebook. When you said, "What a rude driver! Who does he think he is!" and then stew in your bad negative feelings, the Universal secretary wrote down "rude driver who irritates me greatly" in her notebook as well! Isn't that just exhilarating to know? Knowing this is the ultimate personal freedom!

Each time you looked at your debt and cursed it, your impartial Universal secretary would write down "debt" in your notebooks and keep a perfect record of that intention for you. Each time you looked at your bank account balance and worried that it was low, the secretary wrote "low bank balance" in your notebooks and held it perfectly for you. While this is a somewhat humorous analogy, understand that it is how the Universe works! The Universe keeps a perfect record of our intentions and desires until we override or change them.

Without even realizing it, you have created perfect universal records of your dream home, dream job, dream car, dream vacation or dream relationship. How does the Universe even know what your "dream" relationship is like? Well, you have told the Universe over-and-over again, clarified with it over-and-over again through the myriad of relationships that you've had or observed! The Universe has kept perfect records of everything and is continually adding to them.

This is a fundamental Universal truth: The Universe wants very badly to give you whatever you have asked for. It wants to deliver to you everything which you have asked for and recorded in your universal notebooks. But what is the issue here? It can only give you things which match your predominant inner state. Put differently, you only have "access" to the things that match the nature of your current vibrations and thoughts. Therefore at any one time, you are holding yourself vibrationally apart from a lot of the things which you have asked for without even knowing it.

Are you still concerned about how the Universe is going to deliver its good to you, or how it will know what your "good" is?

Give up the need to tell the Universe in great detail what you want or need, because the Universe already *knows!* It has already picked up on the sum total of your thoughts and feelings since the beginning of time! Every single thought or intention which you held has been meticulously curated, just waiting to be delivered to you!

Note how precise these Universal Laws are. The famous inspirational author, Bob Proctor, often quotes the father of our space program, Dr. Wernher von Braun, as saying: "The natural laws of this universe are so precise that we have no difficulty building a spaceship, sending people to the moon and we can time the landing with the precision of a fraction of a second." This is also the famous opening line from the hit Law of Attraction movie *The Secret*. If our universal laws are so precise that they allow us to build marvelous machines, inventions and space-ships, don't you think the Universe has the capabili-ties to hold and accommodate every single one of our minute preferences and desires, right down to the smallest of details?

When you understand this, you understand why the Universe always delivers what you ask for *perfectly*. The Universe does so because it has kept a precise record of your intentions and desires since the beginning of time, and is simply waiting to deliver all of that to you! The moment you have an intention or desire, Universal energy responds perfectly. You create an imprint in the energy field around you. You literally affect the energy field around you. But are you in a position to receive what you have asked for so badly? You will not be in a position to receive if you are vibrationally different, or energetically apart from what you ask for.

This is the reason why the previous exercise of sitting quietly by yourself works so well. When you drop all your negative thoughts and focus on your natural goodness within, you align yourself with the natural vibrations of the Universe. You bring your-self to higher and higher levels of joy, fulfillment, love, and peace. You are coming face-to-face with your true nature and your beingness. It is in *those* moments that you are most receptive to receiving your good because you are in <u>vibrational alignment</u> with all the good things that you have asked for previously!

Therefore, know that you have already done all the asking you need to do. There is no way to physically stop asking. Hence you can never stop creating. You are creating and asking every moment of your life. The Universe is also responding to your asking every time you do so. But are you in a place to receive all the good that has been accumulated and held for you? Do you believe that you can only come in contact with all that good in heaven, or after you die? Do you believe that you need to wait to receive your riches...or would you like to receive them right now?

Receiving them right now is not an act of greed. It is an act of recognition that everything you ask for is already here right now in this moment, waiting to be delivered to you in the most harmonious and straightforward way possible. The only suggestion I can give here is to try this out for yourself. Don't take my word for it. Try all of this out for yourself. No matter what your financial circumstances are, no matter where you have been in the past...drop all of that.

Drop all of that baggage and sit quietly by yourself, becoming aware of the natural goodness that is within you. Feel this goodness and pleasant feeling growing within you. Understand that as these feelings of abundance well up within you that you are not consciously "doing" anything. All you are doing is being yourself. You are being. You are not doing. You are dropping everything that has never been a part of your true nature...all your negative beliefs, thoughts, fears, worries...let all of that go and focus on your pure beingness.

How long should you stay in this inner state? For as long as you like! Stay in this inner state of love and peace because it feels so good for you! You will intuitively know when it is time for you to come out of this state into your normal waking awareness. But the longer you spend in this state, the more profound the changes that will happen to you. Don't turn any of this into work. Just go into the state and stay there. Remember that you are not actively "doing" anything while there. You are just there to notice and perceive the Universal Goodness that has always been there. When you are in that state, you are vibrating at a level that is in line with *all the good things* that you have asked for up to this moment. You are putting yourself in a position to *receive* all that you have asked for.

This is also when the good you seek will start flooding into your experience in ways which you have never imagined. How do I know this so firmly? Why do I have so much conviction that this works? That's because I have experienced all of this intimately. I have seen this working firsthand and producing results in my life when absolutely nothing else worked.

The sheer miracle and beauty of this technique will become apparent once you try it. You don't even have to physically take any outward actions once you have tried this technique. Try it and go to sleep. Or try it and go about your daily life. Try it and stay at home.

You can try what I am describing here and **never venture a single step out of your home**. You can try what I have described here and never make a physical call or have physical contact with another person and <u>things will still manifest for you</u>. Things will <u>find their way to you</u>, simply because space and time are no obstacles for the Universe. Once you clear up what is on the inside, then your outer physical reality *HAS TO BE* transformed in an instant. This is Universal Law. Right now, you may perceive your outer reality to be caused by physical people, things, and events. You may perceive your reality to be the way it is because of external events and happenings.

What I am suggesting to you now (and what you will realize as you deepen your practice) is that all these "external" events, people and things are merely created by our *inner states, thoughts, and feelings*. They have merely been projected onto a big external screen, frame-by-frame, moment-by-moment. Change what goes onto each frame in the projector, and what lights up on the big screen changes in an instant. Stop seeing your current physical reality as cast in stone. Don't even pay any attention to it if it does not please you! Go back repeatedly to the source and stay there. Go back to the field of infinite possibilities in your inner world and stay there...and the Universe will fill the rest of it up perfectly, in a way that is just right for you.

Chapter Eight

Give Up Any Need to Try to be Abundant

What does it take to receive money and abundance into your life? It takes a *willingness* to give up "asking" for money in the first place. Stop asking so hard for the money. The asking is what creates the problem in the first place. Give all of that wanting up. Instead, go deep within into the inner sanctuary and notice the Universal Good that has always been there. In the beginning, this Universal Good will be in the form of mere good feelings. They may not look anything at all like the dollars which you seek, but they *feel* the same. They are broadly of the same vibrational nature and quality, even better than what you can logically conceive in your mind.

So give up the need to ask for money day in and day out. That is keeping you trapped in an endless cycle of limitation. Each time you perceive the need to "ask" for something, you are attached to a certain logical outcome which you have pictured in your mind. You are worried whether you will get it or not. These feelings of worry and attachment cloud your inner state. Feelings of worry and fear are never compatible with the feelings of abundance. Feelings of abundance are feelings of ease, flow, peace and freedom. These feelings can never be found in worry, neither can worrying make any positive manifestations happen.

The natural feelings of abundance are there once you let go of (drop) all your negative, contradictory feelings. They're there once you take off your shades which tinted everything with overriding worry and fear. Take off your shades and see the glorious Universe and the world around you for what it is! Understand that what you are looking at this moment is never inherently *real*. Everything is merely propped up by the energies summoned by your inner state. This is why when I finally understood these teachings, I was able to "give up" most of my worrying at once.

In the past, I would look at the bills I had to pay and worry about whether I had enough money for this month. Then my mind would go into overdrive, making calculations for the next month, and the next. All of this is like getting carried away by a scene in a movie, and allowing your imagination to have power over you. It's silly to do so! The movie has no more power over you than you have power over your inner states.

Once I understood these Universal Principles, the bills and bank account did not morph into something else overnight. They were still the same physically. But the biggest change was in me. I could now look at them differently. I now *know* that they were the manifested results of my *previous* inner states and that my new inner state from this point on would change everything in massive ways. This was all the knowledge and knowing I needed. No outside assurance was necessary. Therefore, in the intervening weeks when I still observed my "old" financial reality, I paid no attention to it. I said, "This is my old reality that is in the process of changing to something better!" I said it, felt it and believed in it because I finally understood these Universal Principles.

Sure enough, within a week or two…physical *signs* started to occur in my reality. They started innocuously enough, in the form of a phone call from an old client wanting to hire me for some work. Then more phone calls and more work opportunities followed. All of this happened <u>without me having to take a single physical action</u>. Please understand that physical action is not the key here. No active, physical intervention is needed on your part. What is needed on your part is <u>mental</u> intervention in the form of letting go of (dropping) all your unwanted negative thoughts and <u>staying there</u>. That is all that is required of you.

Was it easy for me to drop my negative thoughts and stay there in the beginning? Absolutely not! It was downright scary for me. It was scary because my ego mind still kept feeding me all sorts of doomsday scenarios, on what would happen if I did not have money. The ego mind will keep feeding you all this information to keep you "safe." It wants you to "plan" for the future and take preventive measures against unseen dangers. But the ego mind too is acting from its limited physical perspective. It does not know what the Universe knows. It operates in isolation, as an individualistic self, cut off from the Universe. Therefore, the solutions proposed by the ego (and even the rational self) are all based on your physical effort alone. That is why you feel so drained and worn out! We are not in this alone. We are not meant to do this alone.

All through my life, I had come to believe that I was in this alone and had to solve all my financial issues alone. Therefore, everything that I did was predicated on taking action. Everything I did was based on the premise of making something happen through the power of my physical actions and influence. Did it work? To some extent. I achieved *some* results, but obviously still not enough to achieve everlasting abundance and success. In fact, a lot of what I did made me unhappy and wore me out. Of course I was worn out because I was not living by these highest Universal truths! Over time, I allowed myself to believe that I was separate from everyone else and separate from the Universe. Someone who does everything by himself will wear himself out sooner or later.

How are we meant to function in this Universe? In each moment, there are Universal forces standing by and waiting to intervene on our behalf. Universal energy is always flowing through us, whether we realize it or not. When we acknowledge this Universal flow and make use of it, we become one with the

Universal flow. We are no longer struggling against the flow and the tide of things. The Universal flow is what ties everything together. You go along with the Universal flow by letting go of and dropping all your negative, contradictory thoughts that make you feel bad. In the moment you let all of those negative, contradictory feelings go…your sense of well-being and spontaneous joy lets you know that you are moving along with the Universal flow. While it may seem as if you are sitting there, not moving or physically going anywhere, understand that you <u>are</u> at this very moment being swept along the Universal flow!

We are so attached to physical space and physical reality that we look for physical signs of our progress. We look at our surroundings to see if they have changed, or at other tangible signs for "evidence" of our transformation. Doing so will be doing it backward! I have shown you (through the projector analogy) earlier that the same object may be displayed on the screen but made up of many different frames, each holding an image of the same object. Therefore, things are vibrating and progressing so rapidly in every moment that you do not even know it! The reality that is perpetuated stays the same to our physical senses.

When you close your eyes and shift your focus to the inside, you are letting go of negative thoughts, feelings, and beliefs that you have held over a lifetime. Don't even make an effort to let them go. Just close your eyes, turn inwards and notice the spontaneous good feelings that are there. This mere shift of focus would mean you have let them go for the moment. You may feel a profound sense of unconditional joy and exhilaration, far beyond anything which you have experienced before. Not even your best and highest physical achievement could have given you this glorious feeling. Try it for yourself. If you have to do "something," or perceive a need to do "something" about your current situation, then do this and nothing else. Sit quietly by yourself and feel those good feelings intensify. Don't *make* them intensify or try to conjure them up. Remove / drop the words make, do, try or effort from any of this. Instead, replace them with "notice." Simply notice what is there and it will intensify itself for you.

On the outside, it may seem as if you are making little physical progress. It may seem as if you are not moving anywhere. This seems like the most illogical thing to do in the face of pressing problems, which is why so few people ever get down to doing it. As a result, few people have the wisdom of taking this path. I am now cajoling you to do so because trust me; I have tried *everything* humanly possible. If there were a method or technique or spell or "hack" that claimed to bring me more money and prosperity, I would have tried it. I have never found more lasting success than what I am describing to you now.

Each time one of those money spells or hacks worked, the effect was only temporary and sporadic. They did not work as well as I wanted them to. Or I would tire myself out trying to apply them over and over again. I did not achieve everlasting inner peace of mind. Why is that so? Perceiving a *need* to use one of those techniques was a large part of the issue, and then subsequently using them kept me trapped in a state of inner lack. How can we experience abundance in our reality when our inner states are grounded in lack?

From the outside, it seems you are making no progress at all, at least in physical terms. But you are making great *inner* progress. You have just dropped a lifetime of worrying about your finances, or at least reduced it considerably. Remember your Universal secretary from the last chapter? This is when she can do the other half of her work. This is when she can <u>deliver</u> what you have always asked for to you. This is when she can deliver what matches your <u>new inner state</u> to you—which is all the good, money, abundance, prosperity, happiness, wellness and health that you have always wanted.

The Universal Goodness that you experience when you close your eyes and turn inwards signifies your highest and purest connection to the Universe. This is why it feels so good! You perceive, in that moment, the true nature of your being. Only good can come to you when you are in this state because only good will be compatible with you. When you were previously immersed in feelings of constant worry, fear, disappointment and frustration about your finances, only things that matched that could have come to you. But now things are different. All you need to do is to stay there and maintain these Universal good feelings, and all the good you have asked for (in a form individualized for you) will be added to your experience.

You do not have to take my word for this. I have taught this technique to hundreds of thousands of readers over the years. I have done everything I can through the power of the written word and my intention for this series of books. But what is left now is up to you. It is up to you whether you want to turn inwards from this moment on and devote yourself to this new way of thinking and acting in the world.

If you decide to do so (despite your initial skepticism) and persist at it, then the Universe responds in the most beautiful and glorious ways possible. I can assure you that the Universe will surprise and stump you in the most amazing ways. I have no adequate words to convey how the Universe will surprise you because even my most uplifting words are limited by the technicalities of our language.

When the Universal good flows into your life in huge, unbridled, unrestricted ways, you will instinctively understand what I have been talking about. You will finally understand why your previous worries, fears and frustrations about the future have been unfounded.

CHAPTER NINE
DOLLARS FLOW TO YOU EASILY

What is the feeling of dollars flowing to you easily? Before you started this book, you may have thought that this was a feeling you had to conjure up and feel very vividly in your body. You might also have thought that once you found this feeling, you had to work hard at *feeling* it and sustaining it for most of the day. You would have forced yourself to conjure up and feel these feelings as frequently as possible during the day, to "attract" more money into your physical experience.

Now that you have read this book, you finally understand that the feeling of dollars flowing easily to you does not have to be conjured up at all! It does not even have to be forced one single bit. It arises spontaneously within you. No matter where you are, no matter what you are doing…you can turn inwards and notice these feelings on the inside.

The feelings of spontaneous, unconditional peace and joy…that little twinkle on the inside is the feeling of dollars flowing to you easily, at a pace and flow that is just right for you. This feeling does not have to be forced or maintained; it will always be there! How does one begin to acknowledge, recognize and receive this flow? The answer is simple. By paying no attention to what is currently projected on the movie screen on the outside, and by turning your attention inwards to these spontaneous good feelings of joy and peace on the inside. This puts you in a position to receive your greater good.

So I guess in some way, I have mistitled this book. The word "dollars" can be just as easily be replaced with anything and everything good that you want. When you follow this new way of living and acting in the world, one that takes considerable courage in the beginning, you'll find all kinds of good things and experiences being added into your life. You'll find your life becoming more fulfilled and fuller than before, not because you have suddenly become deserving of all your good but because you are now one with everything good that you have asked for all your life. This is the magic of doing all this inner work. The inner work compounds and builds on itself.

Once you notice that the feeling of "dollars flowing easily" is with you every moment of your life, it becomes difficult (if not impossible) to become discouraged by anything that happens on the outside. You know that no matter what happens, you always have constant access to that Universal flow to get back on track again. When you get off-track and see something which you do not like in your physical reality, you immediately understand that it was caused by something in your inner state.

This means you can go back to the source (your inner state of mind) at any time and change it at once. With this realization, nothing will ever throw you off track again. This is why we say once you have understood this new way of living, you would have found everlasting peace and success. Nothing on the outside can affect you! The behavior of other people and things now have no influence over you. You understand that they are merely images projected on the movie screen, as separate as they seem from you. If you don't like what you see, all you have to do is to focus on the Universal Goodness on the inside, and everything straightens itself out.

Some people are worried that their good will not flow to them in sufficient amounts if they do not ask for it or "specify" how much they want. They are still under the impression that they have to "ask" and "beg" the Universe for everything. Give all of this baseless thinking up. The Universe knows everything that you have asked for and everything that you need from the intentions, preferences, and desires that you held in the past (and continue to hold). There is no need to bargain or negotiate with the Universe! The Universe knows what you truly want and delivers it to you, every single time—if you'll put yourself in a place to receive it.

I know of people who need a certain sum of money but will deliberately ask for several times that just in case they do not get what they want. Or they

will ask for extra money "just in case." Give up the
need to engage in any of these lackful actions. A person who asks in this manner is stuck in an inner state
of lackful and limited thinking. He / she wrongly
believes that the Universe will not fulfill all his
desires, therefore, the need to "ask for more," or to
prepare for rainy days. Give up the need to prepare
for rainy days. This does not mean to become irresponsible or to be careless in your spendings, but
simply to take your attention off unwanted future
scenarios. If you want to save money, do so because
it feels good for you and not because you are afraid
of something going wrong. I can't tell you the number of people who have this misplaced mindset of
"saving for a rainy day." Their continued focus on
rainy days virtually guarantees that these days will be
there, waiting for them in future. It is an application
of Universal Laws in reverse!

Before I discovered this new way of living, I was
constantly worried about my finances. I would try
various manifestation techniques to get money and
have some sporadic successes with them. But the
success was never lasting. Something always happened that caused me to spend an unexpected sum
of money here or there. For example, the car would
break down, or an unexpected need had to be met.
All these seemingly external events are merely projections on the outside caused by our inner states.
We are so powerful that we can project our influence onto physical things and events on the outside
and forget that we have done so! The moment I

focused and tended to my inner state, the moment I corrected all of this in my inner state and restored it to a state of love, peace and plenty...everything resolved itself on the outside. The same car that had previously been breaking down and needing expensive repairs ran like a charm. Instead of financial needs to be filled, I found opportunities coming to me, wanting to give me money.

All this is possible once you live the way you have always been meant to—Not to *fight* and push against whatever is happening on the outside, but to recognize that the only work you'll ever have to do is on the inside. If you can focus on those good feelings on the inside and *do nothing else* for the rest of your life, you would still experience the greatest good in your life, in line with your highest desires.

When can you start putting this plan into action? You can start immediately, at any time. You have already started living this way when trying out some of the exercises in the previous chapters. I have set you on a path which you can follow for the rest of your life. But it is up to you whether you want to continue following this path.

In my book *Banned Money Secrets*, I described how I continually and persistently asked for a certain sum of money in my life because I believed having that sum of money would make me feel safe. I kept asking for ten years! Can you imagine yourself asking for something continuously for ten years and not having it in your life? The reason why I was held apart from the fulfillment of my desire for ten years was not because I did not ask hard enough, and not because I did not ask in the right way…but because I was not in a position to receive what I was asking for! How could I receive that sum of money (which to me represented freedom, security and abundance) when my inner state represented lack, worry, and disappointment? All I could receive was only more lack, worry, and disappointment.

Time and tide are never obstacles for the Universe. How long you've had (or not had) something does not even matter for the Universe. What matters is how you are feeling this very moment, and from this point onward. Therefore, this moment in your life is sacred.

The *now* is always sacred. The sooner you realize that you can turn your life around anytime, in this *now* moment…the sooner you'll step into your new desired reality where dollars flow to you easily. Dollars have always been flowing to you easily. Now is your time to receive them. You do not have to wait ten years to receive them like I did. The moment I shifted my focus and stopped asking…the moment I gave up my need to ask and just focused on the eternal goodness within myself here and now, things turned around for me in a few short months!

Can you imagine this? Within a few short months, I received everything I had been asking for during the past decade *and more!* I gave up a decade of struggle in just a few months…and that was because I still did not fully know what I was doing back then.

If I had the full clarity that I am now sharing, things would have turned around even faster.

Rest in the assurance that things are *always* turning around, whether your physical senses can perceive them or not. Right now in this moment, you are the only person who can control what you want your reality to turn *into* next. Only you are in control of that because you are the only person who can drop into and control your own inner state. No one else can do it for you.

Other people may be able to convince you, scare, or even cajole you into action. They may threaten to hurt or harm you, to withdraw certain things in life from you…but once you understand these Universal principles for yourself, everything and everyone else loses their power over you. Once you reclaim this power for yourself (and stop giving it to external people, authority figures, expectations and events), you are free to live and manifest in whatever way you like. Of course, you will still interact and play together with others in your life, but you will do so from a higher level of understanding. You understand that nothing they possibly do can ever hurt or harm you. They can never withhold your good from you, just as you can never withhold their good from them. The only way someone can withhold your good from you is if you wrongly believe that they can, which will cause you to focus all of your attention on their unwanted actions and behaviors.

Give up the belief that your financial good comes from external, physical sources. Each time you are tempted to think that dollars flow to you from your job, from your clients, or from particular opportunities which you have to seize…gently remind yourself that your financial good is already within. There is no need to "seize" anything out there.

If you need positive proof of this, become quiet and turn inwards. Feel the spontaneous good feelings that flow to you in every moment. That is your good flowing to you. This Universal Goodness is so significant because it is *more than just* dollars, it is *beyond* financial abundance. When you realize this, you realize that financial abundance and the dollars you have been asking for are so puny and minuscule compared to the sum total of everything else that has been flowing to you.

Financial riches are only one small part of your well-being, and so much more well-being can flow to you in the form of happy relationships, interactions with others and exhilarating physical experiences. Why limit your good to just dollars by focusing on the money all day long? Why limit your good to just a particular sum of money to meet a particular perceived need? Why limit yourself in these ways? Free yourself from these self-imposed limitations. Free yourself from asking for a specific "sum" just because you think that specific "sum" is what you need, or just the amount you need to feel secure. Leave the details up to the Universe.

When you free yourself from these silly self-imposed limitations, the Universe steps in to give you everything that you have asked for and more.

The "more" is the part that you have forgotten asking for. It is the part that you have asked and denied or convinced yourself that you were not good enough to get. It is the part that you believe you were undeserving to receive. But as we have discussed, belief doesn't even play a part here. Where you focus makes all of the difference. Shift your focus and everything changes in an instant. It doesn't matter for how long or how hard you have been asking. Things can change in the next second, the next minute, the next day or the next week…once you live these truths. The "more" is the part that makes all the difference between just having enough to get by and having plenty.

CHAPTER TEN

YOU HAVE ALREADY TRANSFORMED ON THE INSIDE

Just by reading this book, you would have changed and transformed on the inside. You would already feel lighter and more positive about your financial situation than before. No matter where you were when you first started, you are on your way to recognizing the even greater good in your life. There is no limit to how good this gets. There is nothing *more* you have to do. I hope I have convinced you that there is no money out there that you have to "attract" or "manifest" into your life. All the money you need is already here for your taking. All you need to do is just to *take it* and use it!

As you lay this book down and go about your daily routine, remember my words. Write them down if necessary in a way that resonates with you and keep these reminders of truth close at hand. There will be times when physical evidence will be to the contrary because this physical reality is caused by your old understanding and your old residual feelings. For a short period, your physical reality will still show signs of your old reality. But now you have a choice—Do you want to believe in this old, outdated reality as if it is the ultimate truth, or do you want to exercise your ultimate power as a creator? If you choose the former, you will continue to perpetuate life as it has always been. But if you choose the latter and take me up on my offer, then things will begin changing for you almost immediately. You will see signs of physical manifestation almost immediately *even if* you do not deliberately look out for them. I can assure you that if you follow my instructions to the letter and reduce your worry feelings right down to zero this very moment (which also means paying full attention to the spontaneous Universal Goodness within you), physical manifestations <u>HAVE TO OCCUR</u> even if you do not move a single inch from the chair you're currently sitting in.

You can be sitting in your favorite chair, without having to stand or move a single step…and good things will still happen without your active intervention. This is the part that is so difficult for our egos and for many people to get. All their lives they have been "doing". They have been taking credit for that "doing". They have felt good when they were praised for good results and lousy when they were unappreciated. This is why our ego is so addicted to recognition and fame. The ego always wants others to think that we are the greatest. This is why we have come to place so much emphasis on physical action.

Hopefully, I have convinced you that all the physical action you can take is puny compared to what the Universe can do without your help. This is not to discredit our role as creators, but rather, to illustrate that physical action (the hard work) was never our job in the first place. The physical and non-physical orchestration has always been the Universe's job, never ours. What is our job then? Our job is to decide what we want to create using our free-will, and then to give it up to the Universe to deliver whatever we want to us in the most harmonious ways possible. Our job is to maintain our focus on our inner states until our intentions are fulfilled in our outer reality, *and then* enjoy what we have created from inside ourselves.

If you follow these steps I have outlined, you will find yourself in a positive, self-reinforcing cycle. You will continue to create more and more things that please you, and your attention to those things will cause you to feel even better on the inside. You will observe dollars flowing to you more and more freely on the outside, and this provides positive confirmation of the steps that you have adhered to on the inside.

In a very short time, life will become so good for you, and it will stay that way. You will have no need to worry about bad days or unexpected things happening because there is nothing "unexpected." Everything first takes root in our consciousness (our inner world). When something undesired happens to you, you'll immediately know what caused it on the inside once you have developed a heightened awareness. Even if we accidentally veer off-track, we will know how to get back on track within a very short time. We'll be back on track again even if something manages to throw us off for a moment or two.

When you realize this, what do you have left to fear? No external situation or person can ever have power over you again. So what if you need to start all over again? So what if there is a perceived need to be filled right now in your life, or even several unfilled needs? All of that is illusory and can be changed in an instant. The Universe has already met all your needs not just in a metaphorical way but in a literal manner.

When you turn your focus to the endless flow of abundance on the inside and stay there, you will find that the easy feeling of good (dollars) flowing to you has never diminished. It has been there since the beginning, waiting for you to rediscover the fullness of it.

As you rediscover these feelings within yourself, you will experience an unlimited supply of anything you ask for—abundance, good, money, relationships, and well-being. Stop trying to ask for or attract more. Stop believing that your non-physical good can somehow be exhausted. Stop believing that somehow, what you have asked for may not come to you. How do you add more to something that is already infinite, or subtract something from the wholeness to make it any lesser? You can't. Universal goodness is whole and complete, so will the manifestation of this goodness in your life as riches, abundance and all the good things in your life experience.

There is nothing more you have to *do* to return to this natural state of wholeness and peace. You are already free and complete without realizing it, but in this moment, you are even more acutely aware of this truth than before.

You have effortlessly changed just by gently reading these words and trying the exercises, guided along by your intentions which you consciously or unconsciously hold. This book was born and found its way to you as a result of your personal intentions for greater abundance in your life. Know that even if you never read another word or try another technique again, that everything will still turn out well for you. All has always been well. This is why your good keeps happening through you so long as you keep your highest peace. It is on this note that I wish you peace, and from this peace, all the endless manifestations of abundance in your life. It is done!

ABOUT THE AUTHOR

Richard Dotts is a modern-day spiritual explorer. An avid student of ancient and modern spiritual practices, Richard shares how to apply these timeless principles in our daily lives. For more than a decade, he has experimented with these techniques himself, studying why they work and separating the science from the superstition. In the process, he has created successful careers as an entrepreneur, business owner, author, and teacher.

Leading a spiritual life does not mean walking away from your current life and giving up everything you have. The core of his teachings is that you can lead a spiritual and magical life starting right now, from where you are, in whatever field you are in.

You can make a unique contribution to the world because you are blessed with the abilities of a true creator. By learning how to shape the energy around you, your life can change in an instant if you allow it to!

Richard is the author of more than 20 Amazon bestsellers on the science of manifestation and reality creation. A list of his current books can be found at http://www.RichardDotts.com.

AN INTRODUCTION TO THE MANIFESTATIONS APPROACH OF RICHARD DOTTS

Even after writing more than 20 Amazon bestsellers on the subject of creative manifestations and leading a fulfilling life, Richard Dotts considers himself to be more of an adventurous spiritual explorer than a spiritual teacher or "master," as some of his readers have called him by.

"When you apply these spiritual principles in your own life, you will realize that everyone is a master, with no exceptions. Everyone has the power to design and create his own life on his own terms," says Richard.

"Therefore, there is no need to give up your power by going through an intermediary or any spiritual medium. Each time you buy into the belief that your good can only come through a certain teacher or a certain channel…you give up the precious opportunity to realize your own good. My best teachers were those who helped me recognize the innate power within myself, and kept the faith for me even when I could not see this spiritual truth for myself."

Due to his over-questioning and skeptical nature (unaided by the education which he received over the years), Richard struggled with the application of these spiritual principles in his early years.

After reading thousands of books on related subjects and learning about hundreds of different spiritual traditions with little success, Richard realized there was still one place left unexplored.

It was a place that he was the most afraid to look at: **his inner state.**

Richard realized that while he had been applying these Universal Principles and techniques dutifully on the outside, his inner state remained tumultuous the whole time. Despite being well-versed in these spiritual principles, he was constantly plagued with negative feelings of worry, fear, disappointment, blame, resentment and guilt on the inside during his waking hours. These negative feelings and thoughts drained him of much of his energy and well-being.

It occurred to him that unless he was free from these negative feelings and habitual patterns of thought, any outer techniques he tried would not work. That was when he achieved his first spiritual breakthrough and saw improvements in his outer reality.

Taking A Light Touch

The crux of Richard's teachings is that one has to do the inner work first by tending to our own inner states. No one else, not even a powerful spiritual master, can do this for us. Once we have restored

our inner state to a place of *zero,* a place of profound calmness and peace...that is when miracles
can happen. Any subsequent intention that is held
with <u>a light touch</u> in our inner consciousness quickly
becomes manifest in our outer reality.

Through his books and teachings, Richard
continually emphasizes the importance of taking a
light touch. This means adopting a carefree, play-
ful and detached attitude when working with these
Universal Laws.

"Whenever we become forceful or desperate
in asking for what we want, we invariably delay or
withhold our own good. This is because we start to
feel even more negative feelings of desperation and
worry, which cloud our inner states further and prevent us from receiving what we truly want."

To share these realizations with others, Richard
has written a series of books on various aspects of
these manifestation principles and Universal Laws.
Each of his books touches on a different piece of
the manifestation puzzle that he has struggled with
in the past.

For example, there are certain books that guide
readers through the letting go of negative feelings
and the dropping of negative beliefs. There are
books that talk about how to deal with self-doubt
and a lack of faith in the application of these spiritual principles. Yet other books offer specific techniques for holding focused intentions in our inner
consciousness. A couple of books deal with advanced

topics such as nonverbal protocols for the manifestation process.

Richard's main goal is to break down the mysterious and vast subject of spiritual manifestations into easy to understand pieces for the modern reader. While he did not invent these Universal Laws and is certainly not the first to write about them, Richard's insights are valuable in showing readers how to easily apply these spiritual principles despite leading modern and hectic lifestyles. Thus, a busy mother of three or the CEO of a large corporation can just as easily access these timeless spiritual truths through Richard's works, as an ancient ascetic who lived quietly by himself.

It is Richard's intention to show readers that miracles are still possible in our modern world. When you experience the transformational power of these teachings for yourself, you stop seeing them as unexpected miracles and start seeing them as part of your everyday reality.

Do I have to read every book to create my own manifestation miracles?
Because Richard is unbounded by any spiritual or religious tradition, his work is continuously evolving based on a fine-tuning of his own personal experiences. He does, however, draw his inspiration from a broad range of teachings. Richard writes for the primary purpose of sharing his own realizations and not for any commercial interest, which is why he has

shied away from the publicity that typically comes with being a bestselling author.

All of his books have achieved Amazon bestseller status with no marketing efforts or publicity, a testament to the effectiveness of his methods. An affiliation with a publishing house could mean pressure to write books on certain popular subjects, or a need to censor the more esoteric and non-traditional aspects of his writing. Therefore, Richard has taken great steps to ensure his freedom as a writer. It is this freedom that keeps him prolific.

One of Richard's aims is to help readers apply these principles in their lives with minimal struggle or strain, which is why he has offered in-depth guidance on many related subjects. Richard himself has maintained that there is no need to read each and every single one of his books. Instead, one should just narrow in on the particular aspects that they are struggling with.

As he explains in his own words, "You can read just one book and completely change your life on the basis of that book if you internalized its teachings. You can do this not only with my books but also with the books of any other author."

"For me, the journey took a little longer. One book could not do it for me. I struggled to overcome years of negative programming and critical self-talk, so much so that reading thousands of books did not help me as well. But after I reached that critical tipping point, when I finally 'got it', then I started to get everything. The first book, the tenth book, the hundredth book I read all started to make sense. I could pick up any book I read in the past and intuitively understand the spiritual essence of what the author was saying. But till I reached that point of understanding within myself, I could not do so."

Therefore, one only needs to read as many books as necessary to achieve a true understanding on the inside. Beyond that, any reading is for one's personal enjoyment and for a fine-tuning of the process.

Which book should I start with?

There is no prescribed reading order. Start with the book that most appeals to you or the one that you feel most inspired to read. Each Richard Dotts book is self-contained and is written such that the reader can instantly benefit from the teachings within, no matter which stage of life they are at. If any prerequisite or background knowledge is needed, Richard will suggest additional resources within the text.

OTHER BOOKS
BY RICHARD DOTTS

Many of these titles are progressively offered in various formats (both in hard copy and eBook). Our intention is to eventually make all these titles available in hard copy format.

Please visit http://www.RichardDotts.com for the latest titles and availability.

- **Banned Manifestation Secrets**
  It all starts here! In this book, Richard lays out the fundamental principles of spiritual manifestations and explains common misconceptions about the "Law of Attraction." This is also the book where Richard first talks about the importance of one's inner state in creating outer manifestations.

- **Come and Sit With Me (Book 1): How to Desire Nothing and Manifest Everything**
  If you had one afternoon with Richard Dotts, what questions would you ask him about manifesting your desires and the creative process? In

Come and Sit With Me, Richard candidly answers some of the most pressing questions that have been asked by his readers. Written in a free-flowing and conversational format, Richard addresses some of the most relevant issues related to manifestations and the application of these spiritual principles in our daily lives. Rather than shying away from tough questions about the manifestation process, Richard dives into them head-on and shows the readers practical ways in which they can use to avoid common manifestation pitfalls.

- **The Magic Feeling Which Creates Instant Manifestations**

  Is there really a "magic feeling", an inner state of mind that results in almost instant manifestations? Can someone live in a perpetual state of grace, and have good things and all your deepest desires come true spontaneously without any "effort" on your part? In this book, Richard talks about why the most effective part of visualizations lies in the *feelings*...and how to get in touch with this magic feeling.

- **Playing In Time And Space: The Miracle of Inspired Manifestations**

  In *Playing In Time And Space*, Richard Dotts shares the secrets to creating our own physical reality from our current human perspectives. Instead of seeing the physical laws of space and time as restricting us, Richard shares how anyone can transcend these perceived limitations of space and time by changing their thinking, and manifest right from where they are.

- **Allowing Divine Intervention**
Everyone talks about wanting to live a life of magic and miracles, but what does a miracle really look like? Do miracles only happen to certain spiritual people or at certain points in our lives (for example, at our most desperate)? Is it possible to lead an everyday life filled with magic, miracles, and joy?

 In *Allowing Divine Intervention*, Richard explains how miracles and divine interventions are not reserved for the select few, but can instead be experienced by anyone willing to change their current perceptions of reality.

- **It is Done! The Final Step To Instant Manifestations**
The first time Richard Dotts learned about the significance of the word "Amen" frequently used in prayers...goosebumps welled up all over his body, and everything clicked into place for him. Suddenly, everything he had learned up to that point about manifestations made complete sense.

 In *It Is Done!*, Richard Dotts explores the hidden significance behind these three simple words in the English language. Three words, when strung together and used in the right fashion, holds the keys to amazingly accurate and speedy manifestations.

- **Banned Money Secrets**
In *Banned Money Secrets of the Hidden Rich*, Richard explains how there is a group of individuals in

our midst, coming from almost every walk of life, who have developed a special relationship with money. These are the individuals for whom money seems to flow easily at will, which has allowed them to live exceedingly creative and fulfilled lives unlimited by money. More surprisingly, Richard discovered that there is not a single common characteristic that unites the "hidden rich" except for their unique ability to focus intently on their desires to the exclusion of everything else. Some of the "hidden rich" are the most successful multi-millionaires and billionaires of our time, making immense contributions in almost every field.

Richard teaches using his own life examples that the only true, lasting source of abundance comes from behaving like one of the hidden rich, and from developing an extremely conducive inner state that allows financial abundance to easily flow into your life.

- **The 95-5 Code: for Activating the Law of Attraction**
  Most books and courses on the Law of Attraction teach various outer-directed techniques one can use to manifest their desires. All is well and good, but an important question remains unanswered: What do you do during the remainder of your time when you are not actively using these manifestation techniques? How do you live? What do you do with the 95% of your day, the majority of your waking hours when you are not actively

asking for what you want? Is the "rest of your day" important to the manifestation process?

It turns out that what you do during the 95% of your time, the time NOT spent visualizing or affirming, makes all of the difference.

In *The 95-5 Code for activating the Law of Attraction,* Richard Dotts explains why the way you act (and feel) during the majority of your waking hours makes all the difference to your manifestation end results.

- **Inner Confirmation for Outer Manifestations**
How do you know if things are on their way after you have asked for them?

   What should you do after using a particular manifestation technique?

   What does evidence of your impending manifestations feel like?

   You may not have seen yourself as a particularly spiritual or intuitive person, much less an energy reader...but join Richard Dotts as he explains in *Inner Confirmation for Outer Manifestations* how everyone can easily perceive the energy fields around them.

- **Mastering the Manifestation Paradox**
The Manifestation Paradox is an inner riddle that quickly becomes apparent to anyone who has been exposed to modern day Law of Attraction and manifestation teachings. It is an inner state that seems to be contradictory to the person practicing it, yet one that is associated with

inevitably fast physical manifestations—that of *wanting* something and yet at the same time *not wanting* it.

Richard Dotts explains why the speed and timing of our manifestations depend largely on our mastery of the Manifestation Paradox. Through achieving a deeper understanding of this paradox, we can consciously and deliberately move all our desires (even those we have been struggling with) to a "sweet spot" where physical manifestations *have to occur* very quickly for us instead of having our manifestations happen "by default."

- **Today I Am Free: Manifesting Through Deep Inner Changes**
  In *Today I Am Free*, Richard Dotts returns with yet another illuminating discussion of these timeless Universal Laws and spiritual manifestation principles. While his previous works focused on letting go of the worry and fear feelings that prevent our manifestations from happening in our lives, *Today I Am Free* focuses on a seldom discussed aspect of our lives that can affect our manifestations in a big way: namely our interaction with others and the judgments, opinions and perceptions that other people may hold of us. Richard Dotts shows readers simple ways in which they can overcome their constant feelings of fear and self-consciousness to be truly free.

- **Dollars Flow To Me Easily**
  Is it possible to read and relax your way into financial abundance? Can dollars flow to you

even if you just sat quietly in your favorite arm-chair and did "nothing"? Is abundance and prosperity really our natural birthright, as claimed by so many spiritual masters and authors throughout the ages?

Dollars Flow To Me Easily takes an alternative approach to answering these questions. Instead of guiding the reader through a series of exercises to "feel as if" they are already rich, Richard draws on the power of words and our highest intentions to dissolve negative feelings and misconceptions that block us from manifesting greater financial abundance in our lives.

- **Light Touch Manifestations: How To Shape The Energy Field To Attract What You Want**
  Richard covers the entire manifestation sequence in detail, showing exactly how our beliefs and innermost thoughts can lead to concrete, outer manifestations. As part of his approach of taking a light touch, Richard shows readers how to handle each component of the manifestation sequence and tweak it to produce fast, effective manifestations in our daily lives.

- **Infinite Manifestations: The Power of Stopping at Nothing**
  In *Infinite Manifestations*, Richard shares a practical, step-by-step method for erasing the unconscious memories and blocks that hold our manifestations back. The Infinite Release technique, "revealed" to Richard by the Universe, is a quick and easy way to let go of any unconscious

memories, blocks and resistances that may prevent our highest good from coming to us. When we invoke the Infinite Release process, we are no longer doing it alone. Instead, we step out of the way, letting go and letting God. We let Universal Intelligence decide how our inner resistances and blocks should be dissolved. All we need to do is to intend that we are clear from these blocks that hold us back. Once the Infinite Release process is invoked, it is done!

- **Let The Universe Lead You!**
  Imagine what your life would be like if you could simply hold an intention for something…and then be led clearly and precisely, every single time, to the fulfillment of your deepest desires. No more wondering about whether you are on the "right" path or making the "right" moves. No more second-guessing yourself or acting out of desperation—You simply set an intention and allow the Universe to lead you to it effortlessly!

- **Manifestation Pathways: Letting Your Good Be There…When You Get There!**
  Imagine having a desire for something and then immediately intuiting (knowing) what the path of least resistance should be for that desire. When you allow the Universe to lead you in this manner and unfold the manifestation pathway of least resistance to you, then life becomes as effortless as knowing what you want, planting it

in your future reality and letting your good be there when you get there...every single time! This book shows you the practical techniques to make it happen in your life.

- **And more...**

Made in the USA
Lexington, KY
05 October 2018